For Natalie Heath, with love.

ASTRO
CRYSTALS

STELLA ANDROMEDA

Harness the Power of the Zodiac and the Stones to Manifest the Life You Want

Hardie Grant

BOOKS

PART ONE

PART TWO

PART THREE

PART

ONE

INTRODUCTION

Life has its own momentum and sometimes it can feel
as if we have no power or control over where it leads
us, but this is not true. With a positive mental attitude
you can focus more clearly, and align your energy more
specifically, to manifest those outcomes that support
your hopes and dreams, rather than those that don't.
While positivity is important, banishing all negative
thoughts is impossible – but they can be used as useful
challenges and, as you process negative thoughts, this helps
to focus and overcome mental blocks, enabling you to
manifest what *is* possible.

While that sounds very simple, as if we can change our
lives with a snap of our fingers, the truth lies in authenticity:
we get better results when our lives align with our higher
purpose, when they are right for us. It's not always possible
to see immediately what your higher purpose might be, but
it stems from a belief that to achieve your dreams you need
to access your best intentions. This requires focus and, once
the thinking is clear, the path ahead often reveals itself.
This is the process of manifesting and this in turn can be
enhanced by an understanding and use of crystal energies,
especially those that align to your own zodiac sun sign
(see page 18).

Crystals have long been recognised as beneficial when
it comes to energising or re-energising yourself and
your life's purpose, clearing blockages in your thinking

or your body's chakras and function, and you can work with crystals to manifest positive change in a specific area of life. It may be that you feel blocked in your ability to find happiness in life, perhaps you are repeating old patterns of behaviour that no longer work for you but are seemingly incapable of making a change. Or you may feel stuck at work, not sure that the job you have most closely accords with the person you have become, or are becoming.

You may also feel that you lack the confidence you need to progress as you would like in your relationships with family, friends, work colleagues or lovers. You may be feeling vulnerable in one or other areas of life. Or it may be that your creativity, personal or professional, is blocked in ways you don't quite understand. Wherever we seek pursuit of self-knowledge or change, there are ways in which crystals can help us manifest our purpose.

Many of us are already aware of how each zodiac sun sign (see page 18) relates to a gemstone or crystal that literally embodies our zodiac power. This is information we already have access to and can utilise within our general knowledge of our sun sign qualities. However, there are also a multitude of other possibilities that we can access through a variety of other crystals. Learning how to select and use these is this book's aim, enabling you to work with this additional resource, powering up energy via that of a specific crystal or crystals, secure in the knowledge that you are manifesting the intentions that have your best interests at heart. That you will, by utilising all the positive energy available to you, attract the best of it back to you.

THE LAW OF ATTRACTION

If you want to manifest positive change in your life, you can do this through the law of attraction. The principle of like attracts like, the law of attraction works by putting out positive energy into the world and expecting it back in return. By energising your thoughts and intentions through crystals, you can support positive manifestation of your hopes and desires.

Always punch up, not down and even if you feel negatively about someone or a situation, something you can't actually change, don't let it make you feel powerless: you can always change how you *feel* about it. This in turn empowers you and gives you agency and authenticity in your intention. Putting yourself first in a situation doesn't come easily to many people – but doing so can often help reveal the next steps to manifest your aims, and in turn this can avoid the resentment that blocks energy.

The good news is there is no right or wrong here because working with crystals invokes both the law of attraction (you will choose the stone you need the most at that precise moment) and the law of intention (you will choose the stone that will best help you identify and then manifest your goals and dreams).

To understand the law of attraction, all you need to know is that you will draw to you what you need to focus on and what you spend most time thinking about. And the law of intention works the same way because what you spend your time, energy and money on is what will show up in your life.

These two laws reveal how you can deliberately choose and use your crystals to help create the life you want and to attract the people, resources and opportunities that will help you to achieve your dreams and greatest goals.

Familiarity with crystals and their properties helps you to select those that will energise your intention, by focusing and enhancing the energy around you and by attracting those resources that can manifest those positive outcomes you seek.

Take the time to learn and access these ancient wisdoms of attraction and intention, using crystal energies to enhance your own energy. Then allow those specific crystal energies to help focus your intention to manifest your personal dreams and desires.

ASTROLOGY AND CRYSTALS

Each of us is gifted with a zodiac sun sign, specific to the date of the month we were born, which at its simplest provides us with unique energy that we can utilise or enhance to manifest our intentions. This is the beginning of a journey related to the natural world – the energy of the individual planets, the four elements of air, water, fire and earth, and whether you are a cardinal, fixed or mutable sign, as well as the ancient power of the crystals – and how you relate to it. Bringing a knowledge of all these factors together through positive thought, meditation and intention, will help focus and manifest your hopes, dreams and desires.

THE 12 ZODIAC SIGNS
AND THEIR STONES

Each of the 12 zodiac signs is linked to a precious stone and these provide focus for the sun sign characteristics and their energies, embodying their power. However, not all are crystals and in these cases there are alternatives that will enable you to work with specific energies to manifest your ideas, hopes, dreams and aspirations in accordance with your individual astrological profile.

ARIES

BIRTHSTONE

Diamond

A fire sign often described
as headstrong, with a reputation for
being an instigator, their challenge
is to think before acting and to harness
their ruling Mars energy to continue
with a project even after their initial
enthusiasm begins to wane.

ALTERNATIVE CRYSTALS

Fire Agate, Aventurine,
Carnelian, Red Jasper

✳

Aries is a Cardinal sign

✳

Rules the First Astrological
House of the Self

✳

The head and neck
is ruled by Aries

TAURUS

BIRTHSTONE

Emerald

An earth sign often described
as a lover of beauty and fine things; this
can lead to a lifetime of appreciation,
or to excess. Their challenge is often
to balance these two aspects, enabling
them to garner the best from their
Venus-ruled sensuality.

ALTERNATIVE CRYSTALS

Malachite, Green Tourmaline,
Peridot, Chrysoprase

✳

Taurus is a Fixed sign

✳

Rules the Second Astrological
House of Possessions

✳

The throat, larynx and vocal chords
are ruled by Taurus

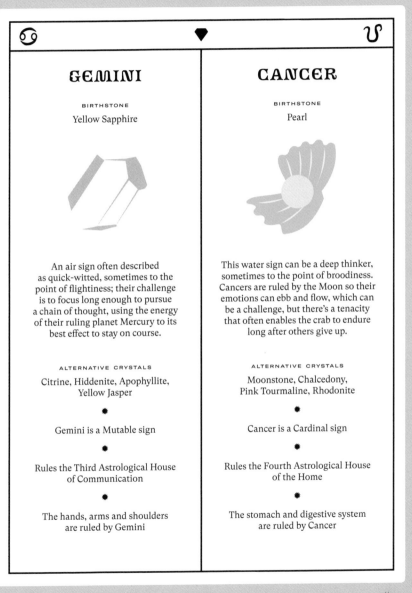

GEMINI

BIRTHSTONE

Yellow Sapphire

An air sign often described as quick-witted, sometimes to the point of flightiness; their challenge is to focus long enough to pursue a chain of thought, using the energy of their ruling planet Mercury to its best effect to stay on course.

ALTERNATIVE CRYSTALS

Citrine, Hiddenite, Apophyllite, Yellow Jasper

✳

Gemini is a Mutable sign

✳

Rules the Third Astrological House of Communication

✳

The hands, arms and shoulders are ruled by Gemini

CANCER

BIRTHSTONE

Pearl

This water sign can be a deep thinker, sometimes to the point of broodiness. Cancers are ruled by the Moon so their emotions can ebb and flow, which can be a challenge, but there's a tenacity that often enables the crab to endure long after others give up.

ALTERNATIVE CRYSTALS

Moonstone, Chalcedony, Pink Tourmaline, Rhodonite

✳

Cancer is a Cardinal sign

✳

Rules the Fourth Astrological House of the Home

✳

The stomach and digestive system are ruled by Cancer

LEO

BIRTHSTONE

Ruby

Larger than life, this fire sign's ego can occasionally be a challenge to those around them and sometimes needs tempering; but like its ruler the Sun, there's no one more loyal or creative or willing to share the excitement and fun of life than Leo.

ALTERNATIVE CRYSTALS

Tiger's Eye, Rose Quartz, Garnet, Red Jasper

*

Leo is a Fixed sign

*

Rules the Fifth Astrological House of Creativity

*

The spine and the heart are ruled by Leo

VIRGO

BIRTHSTONE

Blue Sapphire

This earth sign's attention to detail can verge on perfectionism and their challenge can be to allow their ruling planet Mercury to help them focus on the essential and not get bogged down by the rest, freeing up their innately hard-working nature.

ALTERNATIVE CRYSTALS

Topaz, Moss Agate, Amber, Lapis Lazuli

*

Virgo is a Mutable sign

*

Rules the Sixth Astrological House of Health

*

The nervous system and intestines are ruled by Virgo

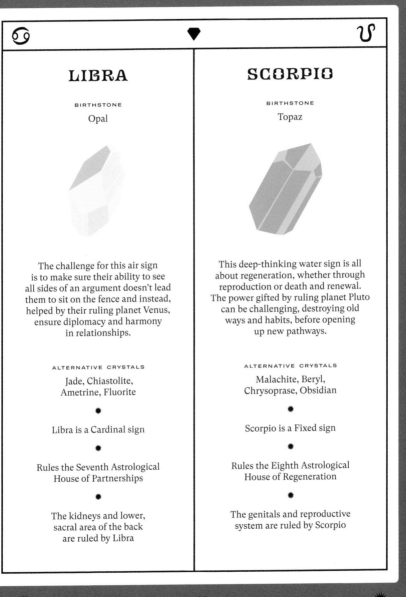

LIBRA

BIRTHSTONE

Opal

The challenge for this air sign is to make sure their ability to see all sides of an argument doesn't lead them to sit on the fence and instead, helped by their ruling planet Venus, ensure diplomacy and harmony in relationships.

ALTERNATIVE CRYSTALS

Jade, Chiastolite, Ametrine, Fluorite

✳

Libra is a Cardinal sign

✳

Rules the Seventh Astrological House of Partnerships

✳

The kidneys and lower, sacral area of the back are ruled by Libra

SCORPIO

BIRTHSTONE

Topaz

This deep-thinking water sign is all about regeneration, whether through reproduction or death and renewal. The power gifted by ruling planet Pluto can be challenging, destroying old ways and habits, before opening up new pathways.

ALTERNATIVE CRYSTALS

Malachite, Beryl, Chrysoprase, Obsidian

✳

Scorpio is a Fixed sign

✳

Rules the Eighth Astrological House of Regeneration

✳

The genitals and reproductive system are ruled by Scorpio

SAGITTARIUS

BIRTHSTONE

Turquoise

Ruled by bountiful Jupiter, this fire sign is all about optimism and escape, and so their challenge can be to recognise a journey's end, staying put long enough to make a commitment, rather than constantly seeking pastures new to explore.

ALTERNATIVE CRYSTALS

Garnet, Labradorite,
Topaz, Tanzanite

✳

Sagittarius is a Mutable sign

✳

Rules the Ninth Astrological House
of Travel

✳

The hips and thighs
are ruled by Sagittarius

CAPRICORN

BIRTHSTONE

Garnet

This pragmatic earth sign can sometimes be burdened by its ruling planet Saturn, the taskmaster of the universe, so the challenge can be to learn to enjoy the view from the mountain as you climb it, relishing the new viewpoints provided.

ALTERNATIVE CRYSTALS

Quartz, Amber, Galena,
Yellow Jasper

✳

Capricorn is a Cardinal sign

✳

Rules the Tenth Astrological House
of Aspirations

✳

The bones and joints
are ruled by Capricorn

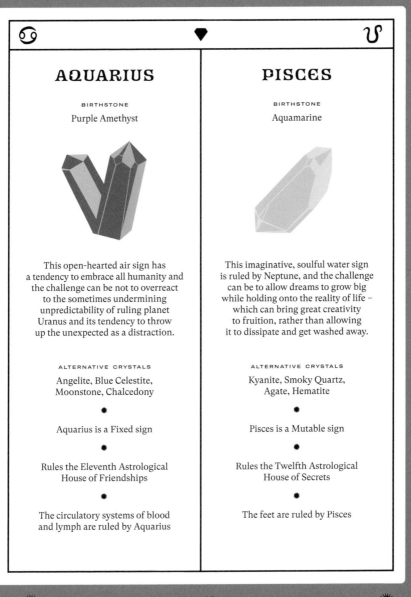

AQUARIUS

BIRTHSTONE

Purple Amethyst

This open-hearted air sign has a tendency to embrace all humanity and the challenge can be not to overreact to the sometimes undermining unpredictability of ruling planet Uranus and its tendency to throw up the unexpected as a distraction.

ALTERNATIVE CRYSTALS

Angelite, Blue Celestite, Moonstone, Chalcedony

✱

Aquarius is a Fixed sign

✱

Rules the Eleventh Astrological House of Friendships

✱

The circulatory systems of blood and lymph are ruled by Aquarius

PISCES

BIRTHSTONE

Aquamarine

This imaginative, soulful water sign is ruled by Neptune, and the challenge can be to allow dreams to grow big while holding onto the reality of life – which can bring great creativity to fruition, rather than allowing it to dissipate and get washed away.

ALTERNATIVE CRYSTALS

Kyanite, Smoky Quartz, Agate, Hematite

✱

Pisces is a Mutable sign

✱

Rules the Twelfth Astrological House of Secrets

✱

The feet are ruled by Pisces

THE POWER OF CRYSTALS

Like many other objects, crystals have their own unique vibrational energy, which can be measured and quantified. Long before it was possible to do this, crystals were seen as protective talismans by civilisations like ancient Egypt and China, while many cultures today continue to revere the perceived power of the stones.

We have our own vibrational energy that can become depleted or blocked, and crystals can help us to revive or re-energise our bodies and minds. We each have seven primary energy centres or chakras (see page 31) and there are different crystals that specifically relate to each of these. Working with this knowledge is a good starting point to understanding the power of the crystal.

Crystals help to focus energy and in turn can be used to enhance or balance your own energy. Different crystals have different properties and choosing an appropriate crystal to use is an art as much as a science.

In addition, a crystal often resonates with someone's energy in a positive way and they will feel automatically drawn to selecting it, with a strongly intuitive feeling that this one is the one they need.

Once you become familiar with the different properties of specific crystals (see Part Three) you can utilise these for the outcomes you want to manifest, either individually or in combination, through meditation or just by having them close to hand on your person or in your home. The beauty of crystals is that their energetic, vibrational resonance is akin to our own, and their use is available to us all.

CRYSTALS FOR CHAKRAS

The literal translation for the Sanskrit word 'chakra' is 'wheel', and each of the seven chakras of the body relates to a focus of energy. When your primary chakras are blocked, then energy can't vibrate or flow freely through the body or between these power points, and you can feel low and negative in energy. Working with crystals can help focus, realign and power up your energy at each of the seven major chakras. Different crystals have the energetic resonance that relates to a particular chakra, so it's useful to know what these are and use them accordingly in application, meditation or affirmation.

CROWN

Imagine a bright white cord coming down from the heavens bringing pure energy into your body via the top of your head. This is your crown chakra.

CROWN CHAKRA CRYSTALS

amethyst and/or clear quartz

CROWN CHAKRA MEDITATION

'I Understand'

Hold your chosen crystal in the centre of your chest so it can connect your heart with your crown chakra and repeat this beautiful affirmation:

AFFIRMATION

I understand all that is, all that was and all that ever will be.

COLOUR

In your mind's eye, see the colour (or non-colour) white.

THIRD EYE

Located in the centre of your forehead, between the eyebrows, your third eye is often called the seat of your intuition. As you develop spiritually you will feel this chakra opening up.

THIRD EYE CHAKRA CRYSTALS
fluorite and/or moonstone

THIRD EYE CHAKRA MEDITATION

'I See'

Bring your hands together into prayer, fingers and thumbs pressing together and then lift your hands to your third eye chakra.

Place your chosen crystal in your lap so it is physically connected with your body and repeat this third eye chakra affirmation:

AFFIRMATION
I see the Unseen. I know the Unknown.

COLOUR
In your mind's eye, see the colour purple.

THROAT

Your throat chakra lies in the centre of your throat. This chakra is often blocked because we are expected to 'follow the herd' and keep any controversial views to ourselves.

THROAT CHAKRA CRYSTALS
lapis lazuli and/or blue celestite

THROAT CHAKRA MEDITATION

'I Speak Out'

Gently feel into your throat chakra with your finger and become aware of the power of the voice – your voice – that lies there; often silenced by others or your own fear of disapproval.

Either hold your chosen crystal in your hand and close your eyes, or gaze at the crystal as you repeat this throat chakra affirmation:

AFFIRMATION
I will speak my truth. I will no longer hide what I truly think.

COLOUR
In your mind's eye, see the colour blue.

HEART

Your heart chakra lies in the middle of your upper chest, in the centre of the breastbone. This is also an important calming energy portal known as The Sea of Tranquillity.

HEART CHAKRA CRYSTALS
rose quartz and/or aventurine.

HEART CHAKRA MEDITATION

'I Love'

Feel universal and unconditional love flowing in and out of the heart centre as you connect with this chakra. Know that you are and always will be deeply loved.

Either hold your chosen crystal in your hand and close your eyes, or gaze at the crystal as you repeat this heart chakra affirmation:

AFFIRMATION
I am open to love. I offer all my love. I receive your love.

COLOUR
In your mind's eye, see the colour pink or green.

SOLAR PLEXUS

Your solar plexus chakra sits in the lower abdominal region, a few fingers down from your navel. This chakra is home to your personal power and helps you take action.

SOLAR PLEXUS CHAKRA CRYSTALS
citrine and/or turquoise

SOLAR PLEXUS CHAKRA MEDITATION

'I Do'

As you connect to the energy centre it supports what you need to do to manifest the life changes you want and to draw to you what will make that happen.

Either hold your chosen crystal in your hand and close your eyes, or gaze at the crystal as you repeat this solar plexus chakra affirmation:

AFFIRMATION
I have the power. I have the know-how. I am ready for action.

COLOUR
In your mind's eye, see the colour orange.

SACRAL

Your sacral chakra sits in the pelvic region around the sex organs and is the energy centre that governs and enhances your creativity.

SACRAL CHAKRA CRYSTALS

amber and/or carnelian

SACRAL CHAKRA MEDITATION

'I Feel'

As you connect to the energy centre that governs creativity, including physical reproduction, imagine this energy store is available to support your creativity.

Either hold your chosen crystal in your hand and close your eyes, or gaze at the crystal as you repeat this sacral chakra affirmation:

AFFIRMATION

I am in tune. I am in the flow. I can create.

COLOUR

In your mind's eye, see the colour yellow.

ROOT

Your root chakra sits at the base of your spine and is the energy centre that keeps you grounded and connected to the earth.

ROOT CHAKRA CRYSTALS

obsidian and/or tourmaline

ROOT CHAKRA MEDITATION

'I Am'

Imagine spirals of energy flowing from the base of your spine down through the ground connecting to the earth and then back up into your body again.

Either hold your chosen crystal in your hand and close your eyes, or gaze at the crystal as you repeat this root chakra affirmation:

AFFIRMATION

I am grounded. I am stable. I am connected.

COLOUR

In your mind's eye, see the colour red swirling around this energy centre.

YOUR AURA

Everybody's body has an energy field with its own
vibrational energy, made up of your physical body,
your feelings, your spiritual heart and your cosmic being.
This energetic field is also known as your aura, and
while it is invisible to most, some psychics and holistic
health practitioners can see the type, colour and quality
of vibrational energy of a person's aura. They can tell
from the aura whether someone's energy is balanced
or blocked, healthy or in need of realignment.

There are seven aural planes, different levels of energy, each with a specific function.

PHYSICAL PLANE

This is your physical body, and the layer closest to your skin.

EMOTIONAL PLANE

This relates to your feelings, and how you are feeling; if you are happy, sad or depressed, it will show up here.

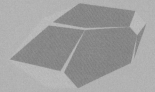

ASTRAL PLANE

This plane stores your capacity for love and is your spiritual level.

MENTAL PLANE

This is the level of rational and intellectual reasoning, it's where you are most logical.

ETHERIC PLANE

This is where you are most intuitive and in some cases, psychic, able to connect with other people's energy.

CAUSAL PLANE

This level harmonises all the others and is the focus of inspiration for your life's path.

CELESTIAL PLANE

Here you store your most creative thoughts, dreams and ideas and this is the level of enlightenment.

These seven levels relate to the seven chakras (see page 31) and these vibrational energies can be positively affected by crystal energies, which can be used to heal and protect the aura. Holistic health practitioners who work with the aura can help you, but with a working knowledge of the crystals you will be able to rebalance, re-align or unblock your own aura to promote emotional and physical health and healing.

PART

THE CRYSTALS AND THEIR QUALITIES

Everything around us and everything within us is made up of energy. And this applies to crystals; each will have its own specific energy and so working with crystals is a way of using their vibrational energy to enhance or calm your own. You can use the stones to raise or lower the vibration energy in your body, your home, at your desk, on your yoga mat or during meditation, depending on what you want to achieve.

Different crystals have different qualities that can be used to energise aspects of our being, body and mind and at a spiritual level. You can think of the crystals that you bring into your life to work with as being like guides or allies on your journey. And while the crystal you hold in your hand is a solid structure – just like a table or a chair – what you will be working with are the vibrational energies of that specific crystal.

Crystal healers talk about the Dominant Oscillatory Rate (DOR) of a crystal – what this means is that every stone will vibrate at a consistent rate, regardless of what you do to it or where you place it. This is because crystals are made up of atoms and molecules that repeat themselves in a rigid structure, and so even as the crystal grows this remains consistent. This stability is unique, and it is what we are working with when we utilise a particular crystal.

Unlike a stable crystal, however, your own body's energy fluctuates; it doesn't vibrate at either the same or a consistent rate. If you feel scared or excited, your heartbeat goes up and your breath shortens, which means your heart and lungs have changed their energetic frequency. When you feel calm and happy, your brainwave pattern slows down, as does your breathing, and so again, your personal Dominant Oscillatory Rate (DOR) has changed. It fluctuates, depending on what is happening in both your internal and external worlds. But you can use the stability of a crystal's vibrational energy to change your energy to your advantage, once you know how.

When you hold the crystal you'e chosen for a specific purpose, your body's energy responds to its vibration and starts to synchronise with that of the crystal. And by doing this, the crystal can then confer its healing or spiritual properties to you – whether you are seeking to be more creative, to find your voice in order to express yourself more confidently, or to heal from the trauma of illness, an accident or surgery. That crystal will be your ally, enabling you to focus on and manifest your deepest desire and dreams.

It is, of course, true that the more you study the crystals and what they have to offer, the more you will make an informed choice about which crystals you want to work with at any given time. But you can also choose to start with those crystals that are known to resonate with your astrological birth sign (see page 18), or you can trust your intuition and select the crystal you feel most drawn to on sight, and then research its properties to find out why that was the case for you.

There is no right or wrong here because working with crystals invokes both the law of attraction (see page 13) – you will choose the stone you need the most at that precise moment – and the law of intention (see page 14) – you will choose the stone that will best help you identify and then manifest your goals and dreams.

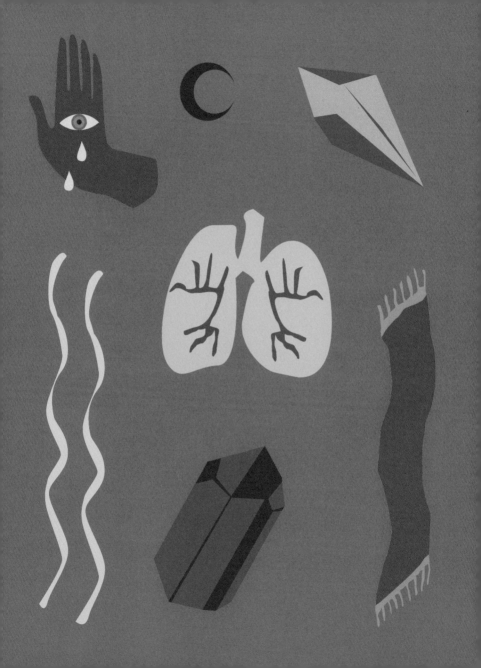

CHOOSING YOUR CRYSTALS

When it comes to choosing your crystals the best guide you will ever have – and the only one you ever really need – is your own intuition. And the way you do this could not be more simple – if you find yourself looking at a selection of crystals just follow your gut and pick the one that you feel you are most drawn to.

If there is a short description of the properties of that particular stone available to you, read it and see what resonates most strongly with you. If, for instance, you are reading about Blue Celestite – which connects us with the higher realms – and you feel your heart skip a beat with excitement, this is a sign that this is a crystal you should be working with.

You can also select specific crystals that will help balance out your own character traits and feelings. If, for example, you are indecisive, choose a crystal such as Clear Quartz, which brings great clarity. And if you are just starting out, then keep things simple and choose your first precious stone based on your Zodiac sign (see page 18).

You can also choose
your stones based
on their shapes using
the following guidance:

SINGLE POINTED

Directs energy one way so fantastic to
place in the middle of your crystal circle.

WAND SHAPE

Use to command the energy
of the stone.

DOUBLE POINTED

Directs energy in two directions.
This shape is important in circle work
because you can direct the energy
back to your focus stone and out
to the Universe.

PYRAMID SHAPE

Represents all sides of a situation
with the truth at the centre.

PALM STONES

These are calming and comforting,
to hold in your hand.

CARVED ANIMAL SHAPES

Bring the healing properties
of those spirit animals.

HEART-SHAPED STONES

Brings romance and loving kindness.

ARROW-SHAPED

Accelerates the rate
of healing and can be used
to cut toxic cords.

COLOUR

An intrinsic factor of the vibrational energy of crystals is their colour, so it's worth remembering that just the colour of your chosen crystal will have an effect. This relates in part to your chakras (see page 31) but you can also make your choices based on this general guidance.

PURPLE

Spiritually healing and calming, also aids intuition.

WHITE

Purity of thought and meditative process.

BLUE

Soothing and calming.

GREEN

Promotes a sense of groundedness, particularly in mental activity.

ORANGE

Promotes creativity and energy.

YELLOW

Uplifting and dispels negativity.

RED

Stimulates the body and mind.

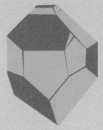

CRYSTALS IN THE HOME

Along with their use for particular purposes, intentions, rituals or manifestations, you can place crystals around your home to boost or unblock energy in stagnant areas or to generally utilise a crystal's properties to improve your environment. A single stunning crystal, or as part of a collection, not only radiates its energy: it can also be a beautiful addition to your domestic environment. The following are just suggestions, but as you develop your skills in using crystals, you will discover what works best for you and your surroundings.

BATHROOM

AMBER
soothes
inflammation

MOONSTONE
aligns with the lunar cycle

TURQUOISE
supports inner harmony

BEDROOM

AGATE
balances emotional
and physical energy

ROSE QUARTZ
promotes feelings of joy

LAPIS LAZULI
helpful to loving communication

SITTING ROOM

AMETHYST

promotes relaxation

AVENTURINE

soothes anger and irritation

PERIDOT

encourages optimism

KITCHEN

CARNELIAN
imparts confidence

JADE
attracts luck

FLUORITE
neutralises negative energy

OFFICE

CITRINE
aids creativity

CLEAR QUARTZ
strengthens your intentions

HEMATITE
draws away negative energy

CARING FOR YOUR CRYSTALS

Keep your crystals in a safe place, perhaps in a soft cloth bag or lined box, to avoid chipping, scuffing or accidentally damaging them. Some crystals have a natural affinity to each other and can be kept together, or you may wish to keep them in individual containers.

Continual use, or carrying crystals on your body for extended periods, can sometimes reduce their vibrational energy so it can be useful to rest and recharge your crystals from time to time. You can do this by putting them in a small ceramic or glass (don't use plastic) container of distilled, or rainwater with a sprinkle of sea salt, and placing them either in full sunlight for several hours or overnight in the moonlight.

POWERING UP YOUR CRYSTALS

Choose a crystal by focusing on the properties you wish to bring to yourself, your home or your work space, and concentrate on how you respond to it as you hold it. Take a few peaceful moments to meditate on, and more deeply connect, with the crystal you've chosen and power it up in the following way.

Hold the crystal in your non-dominant hand,
close your eyes and breathe in long, slow
deep breaths, which help calm both the mind
and the body.

Take your focus inwards and begin
to connect with the crystal, which will
already be radiating its energy in your hand.

Really try to feel the quality of this
stone's energy. Try to visualise its power.

Now visualise precisely how you would like
the crystal's energy to work. Clearly state what
you need: try saying it aloud or writing it down.

Once you have clarified and stated your
intention, focus on the crystal and return
your breathing to normal.

Then take six long, deep breaths, open
your eyes and end your meditation.

USING CRYSTALS
TO MANIFEST

Be clear about what you want. Your chosen crystals
are your tangible and stable allies, working with you
to attract more of what you want and need in your life.
But when you work with them, you need to be crystal
clear about what it is you want and then make sure
you are using the right crystal to support that ambition
or goal.

If for instance, you would like a new relationship,
spend some time thinking about what that might look
like before diving in to ask for it. Are you looking for
something casual and light-hearted or are you ready
for a big commitment with someone who shares your
values and life goals?

When it comes to work, do you want to continue
on your current path or make a complete change?
Or perhaps you want to shift sideways, taking your
unique skills, experience or expertise into a new arena.
Or maybe you just want to achieve a promotion and
are not sure how to go about it. You may be looking

to enhance your creativity in a particular project. Alternatively, perhaps you need to support your health during or after illness or accident – whatever it is, be specific, so that the crystal can help you manifest what you need or want.

What can be helpful in clarifying what you want is to list the pros and cons, in order to be really focused. Taking some time at this stage to really work out what you want to happen in your life always helps to yield a better outcome.

SET YOUR INTENTION

Setting your intent is always the first step in getting what you want in life. The crystals have plenty of superpowers, but mind-reading isn't one of them, so you need to spell out what you are asking for. You don't have to explain why, there's no judgement here and no need to justify your deepest heart-felt desires.

One of the best ways to set an intent is to light a candle and either say out loud what you want to happen or write it down and leave it (safely) beside or underneath the candle as the flame burns out. There's no need to splash out or go to town – you can use a simple tea light on a saucer if you don't have a fancy candle and holder. What matters here is the seriousness of your intent.

It can sometimes feel a bit awkward trying to think of the right words to say when you want to set an intent and you may initially feel a bit self-conscious talking as you focus on a candle flame in an empty room. But your crystals are already charged and powered up to help change your vibration to attract what you most want.

CRYSTAL MEDITATIONS

Taking a moment to focus on your crystals through meditation can help you in the manifestation of your intent. The suggestions below will help you focus and, in time and as you get more used to your crystals, you will come to know what words to use and say.

TO ATTRACT LOVE

LIGHT YOUR CANDLE, CLOSE YOUR EYES AND EITHER SAY OUT LOUD (OR SILENTLY REPEAT) THE WORDS:

My heart is open to both giving and receiving love in its highest forms.

✳

I am ready to meet my love and share my life with them.

✳

I am ready to meet my love and share their life with them.

✳

I am open. I am ready.

TO ATTRACT MEANINGFUL WORK

LIGHT YOUR CANDLE, CLOSE YOUR EYES AND EITHER SAY OUT LOUD (OR SILENTLY REPEAT) THE WORDS:

I offer myself and my talents to the service of the greater good.

✷

I am ready to take on more meaningful work.

✷

I am asking for work that makes a positive difference in the world.

✷

I am ready to start now.

TO ATTRACT ABUNDANCE

LIGHT YOUR CANDLE, CLOSE YOUR EYES AND EITHER SAY OUT LOUD (OR SILENTLY REPEAT) THE WORDS:

I am open to the bounty of the Universe.

✷

I understand the only limitations on the abundance of life are those I have placed on myself.

✷

I am worthy of abundance.

✷

I pledge to do my best to share that abundance so it can flow freely to and from me.

CRYSTAL CIRCLES

Another way of amplifying the power of your crystals is by creating a circle, using different crystals that work together to direct all their energy and focus it on your stated intent. This is a creative endeavour that you can think of as being a kind of crystal artwork for your home. This four-step example will show how best to use crystals in this way, but as you become more confident and experienced with working with crystals you can create your own circle.

STEP 1

SET YOUR INTENTION

For example: I want to have the courage to speak up and make my point more clearly.

STEP 2

CHOOSE YOUR STONES

You need to select crystals that have the properties you want to amplify or enhance their power. For example, you might choose Rose Quartz to help your heart open with self-love as you dig for the courage to speak out. You may also want to include a crystal such as Fluorite for better communication and then a crystal-like Blue Celestite that will connect you with those who can support you through this transition.

STEP 3
CREATE YOUR CIRCLE

Place your chosen crystal at the centre of your circle and arrange the others around it. Use between 6–12 stones, all of which are chosen to bring some assistance to achieving your goal of finding and using your true voice. Place these stones equidistant from each other and from your central focus stone that they encircle. You may want to choose a Clear Quartz for this central focus because this is a crystal that will amplify the properties of the other stones in the circle.

STEP 4
ACTIVATE YOUR CIRCLE OF CRYSTALS

You use your voice to activate the circle and state out loud your intention. You can also move the stones in and out of the circle space to activate and amplify the properties they impart.

The more familiar you become with using crystals in your life, the more comfortable and trusting you will feel about their use. Initially, taking the time to consciously think about what you want to use the crystals to manifest can feel strange, but with familiarity you will learn to trust your intuition and the outcomes you manifest through their use. Like any journey, it begins with some simple steps and with crystals; choosing those that speak to you most clearly and with which you feel most comfortable is the first step. Then your crystals will become something you really can trust.

PART

THREE

INTRODUCTION

When it comes to putting your crystals to use, there
will be particular areas in which you want to manifest
your hopes and desires and so it can be especially
useful to have a guide to the range of crystals that can
be used alone, or in association with others in a circle
manifestation (see page 72). You already have your zodiac
gemstones and crystals available to you (see page 18),
but a closer understanding of a particular crystal's
properties and usefulness for manifesting a particular
outcome can help you understand and make the best
use of the selection you have.

The following sections look at eight different areas
of application – Love, Confidence, Health, Creativity,
Work Success, Happiness, Fertility and Protection –
and each of the eight crystals for each section has been
specifically selected for what its properties can bring
to realising your intention. Utilising these will help
focus the energies you need to manifest the outcomes
you wish for. As you become more skilled in your use
of crystals, you will find their properties will reveal
themselves more clearly, so it's always worth listening
to your inner voice whenever you are working with
your crystals.

CRYSTALS FOR LOVE

We love in many different ways. There is the love we feel for our family, our children and our friends, which is very different to how we might feel about an intimate partner or lover. The ancient Greeks identified these different forms as 'eros' or 'erotic love', 'agape' or 'love of mankind', 'philia' or 'the love of friends or equals', and 'storge' or 'familial and unconditional love'. There is also philautia or self-love, which is a very good place to start – loving ourselves first makes it easier to love others.

You will know where you want to focus your intention and what you want to manifest when it comes to accessing the properties of the eight crystals selected here for love. Make sure you are clear on your intention (see page 66) before you start.

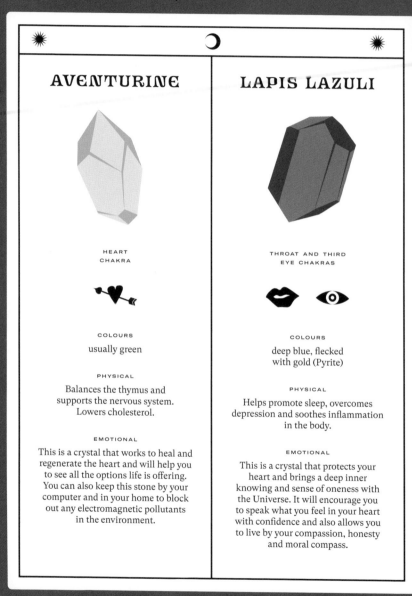

AVENTURINE

HEART
CHAKRA

COLOURS

usually green

PHYSICAL

Balances the thymus and
supports the nervous system.
Lowers cholesterol.

EMOTIONAL

This is a crystal that works to heal and
regenerate the heart and will help you
to see all the options life is offering.
You can also keep this stone by your
computer and in your home to block
out any electromagnetic pollutants
in the environment.

LAPIS LAZULI

THROAT AND THIRD
EYE CHAKRAS

COLOURS

deep blue, flecked
with gold (Pyrite)

PHYSICAL

Helps promote sleep, overcomes
depression and soothes inflammation
in the body.

EMOTIONAL

This is a crystal that protects your
heart and brings a deep inner
knowing and sense of oneness with
the Universe. It will encourage you
to speak what you feel in your heart
with confidence and also allows you
to live by your compassion, honesty
and moral compass.

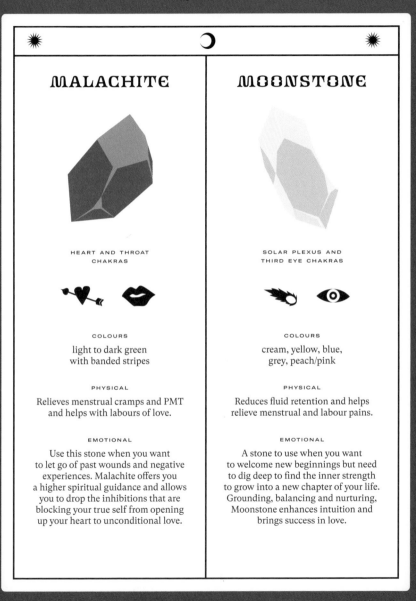

MALACHITE

HEART AND THROAT CHAKRAS

COLOURS

light to dark green
with banded stripes

PHYSICAL

Relieves menstrual cramps and PMT
and helps with labours of love.

EMOTIONAL

Use this stone when you want
to let go of past wounds and negative
experiences. Malachite offers you
a higher spiritual guidance and allows
you to drop the inhibitions that are
blocking your true self from opening
up your heart to unconditional love.

MOONSTONE

SOLAR PLEXUS AND THIRD EYE CHAKRAS

COLOURS

cream, yellow, blue,
grey, peach/pink

PHYSICAL

Reduces fluid retention and helps
relieve menstrual and labour pains.

EMOTIONAL

A stone to use when you want
to welcome new beginnings but need
to dig deep to find the inner strength
to grow into a new chapter of your life.
Grounding, balancing and nurturing,
Moonstone enhances intuition and
brings success in love.

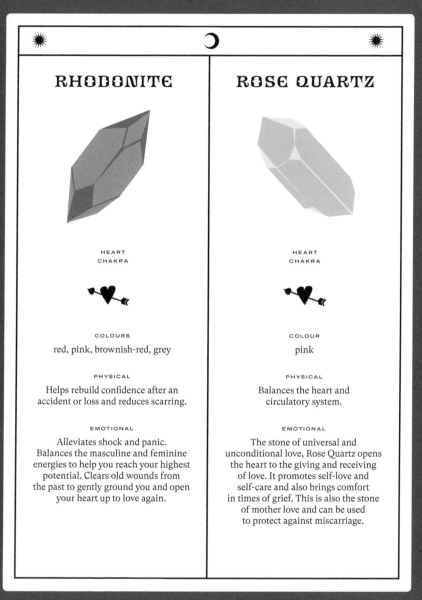

RHODONITE

HEART
CHAKRA

COLOURS
red, pink, brownish-red, grey

PHYSICAL
Helps rebuild confidence after an
accident or loss and reduces scarring.

EMOTIONAL
Alleviates shock and panic.
Balances the masculine and feminine
energies to help you reach your highest
potential. Clears old wounds from
the past to gently ground you and open
your heart up to love again.

ROSE QUARTZ

HEART
CHAKRA

COLOUR
pink

PHYSICAL
Balances the heart and
circulatory system.

EMOTIONAL
The stone of universal and
unconditional love, Rose Quartz opens
the heart to the giving and receiving
of love. It promotes self-love and
self-care and also brings comfort
in times of grief. This is also the stone
of mother love and can be used
to protect against miscarriage.

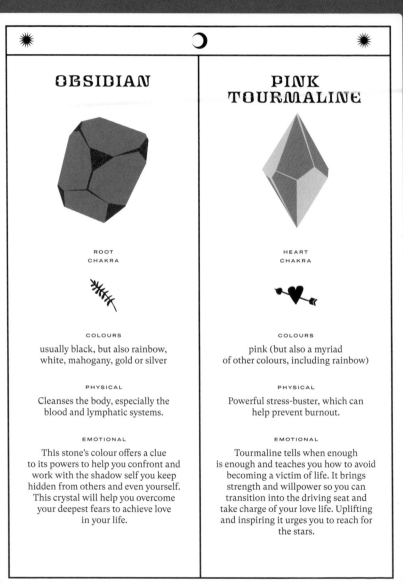

OBSIDIAN

ROOT
CHAKRA

COLOURS

usually black, but also rainbow,
white, mahogany, gold or silver

PHYSICAL

Cleanses the body, especially the
blood and lymphatic systems.

EMOTIONAL

This stone's colour offers a clue
to its powers to help you confront and
work with the shadow self you keep
hidden from others and even yourself.
This crystal will help you overcome
your deepest fears to achieve love
in your life.

PINK TOURMALINE

HEART
CHAKRA

COLOURS

pink (but also a myriad
of other colours, including rainbow)

PHYSICAL

Powerful stress-buster, which can
help prevent burnout.

EMOTIONAL

Tourmaline tells when enough
is enough and teaches you how to avoid
becoming a victim of life. It brings
strength and willpower so you can
transition into the driving seat and
take charge of your love life. Uplifting
and inspiring it urges you to reach for
the stars.

CRYSTALS FOR CONFIDENCE

Some days even the most confident of us can struggle with confidence. Some days you need some extra help, perhaps because you have to interview for a job, deliver a speech, take an exam or communicate something difficult to someone. Whatever the need, there is the possibility of improving or enhancing your self-confidence, either specifically or in general, and manifesting the outcome you need or want.

You will know where you want to focus your intention and what you want to manifest when it comes to accessing the properties of the eight crystals selected here for confidence. Make sure you are clear on your intention (see page 66) before you start.

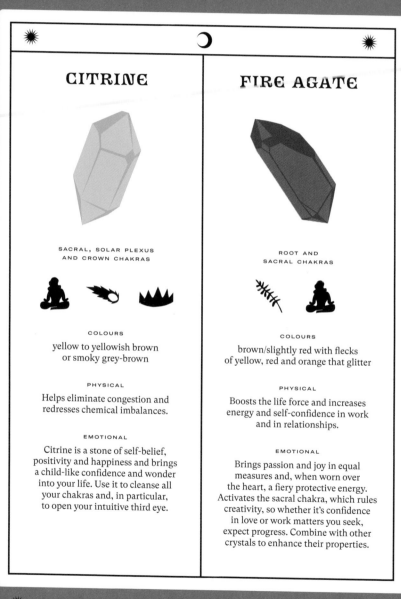

CITRINE

SACRAL, SOLAR PLEXUS
AND CROWN CHAKRAS

COLOURS

yellow to yellowish brown
or smoky grey-brown

PHYSICAL

Helps eliminate congestion and
redresses chemical imbalances.

EMOTIONAL

Citrine is a stone of self-belief,
positivity and happiness and brings
a child-like confidence and wonder
into your life. Use it to cleanse all
your chakras and, in particular,
to open your intuitive third eye.

FIRE AGATE

ROOT AND
SACRAL CHAKRAS

COLOURS

brown/slightly red with flecks
of yellow, red and orange that glitter

PHYSICAL

Boosts the life force and increases
energy and self-confidence in work
and in relationships.

EMOTIONAL

Brings passion and joy in equal
measures and, when worn over
the heart, a fiery protective energy.
Activates the sacral chakra, which rules
creativity, so whether it's confidence
in love or work matters you seek,
expect progress. Combine with other
crystals to enhance their properties.

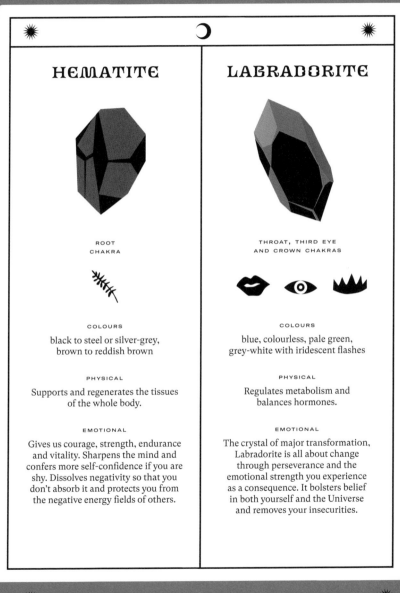

HEMATITE

ROOT
CHAKRA

COLOURS

black to steel or silver-grey,
brown to reddish brown

PHYSICAL

Supports and regenerates the tissues
of the whole body.

EMOTIONAL

Gives us courage, strength, endurance
and vitality. Sharpens the mind and
confers more self-confidence if you are
shy. Dissolves negativity so that you
don't absorb it and protects you from
the negative energy fields of others.

LABRADORITE

THROAT, THIRD EYE
AND CROWN CHAKRAS

COLOURS

blue, colourless, pale green,
grey-white with iridescent flashes

PHYSICAL

Regulates metabolism and
balances hormones.

EMOTIONAL

The crystal of major transformation,
Labradorite is all about change
through perseverance and the
emotional strength you experience
as a consequence. It bolsters belief
in both yourself and the Universe
and removes your insecurities.

OBSIDIAN

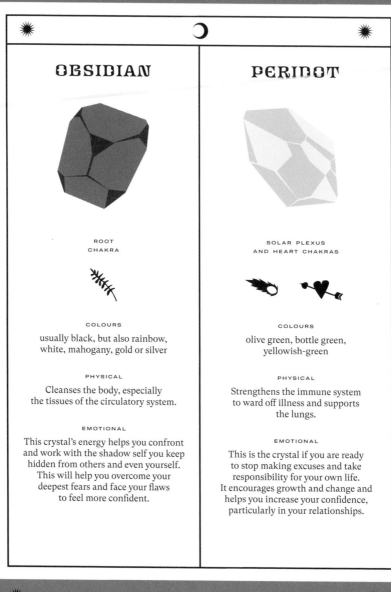

ROOT
CHAKRA

COLOURS

usually black, but also rainbow,
white, mahogany, gold or silver

PHYSICAL

Cleanses the body, especially
the tissues of the circulatory system.

EMOTIONAL

This crystal's energy helps you confront
and work with the shadow self you keep
hidden from others and even yourself.
This will help you overcome your
deepest fears and face your flaws
to feel more confident.

PERIDOT

SOLAR PLEXUS
AND HEART CHAKRAS

COLOURS

olive green, bottle green,
yellowish-green

PHYSICAL

Strengthens the immune system
to ward off illness and supports
the lungs.

EMOTIONAL

This is the crystal if you are ready
to stop making excuses and take
responsibility for your own life.
It encourages growth and change and
helps you increase your confidence,
particularly in your relationships.

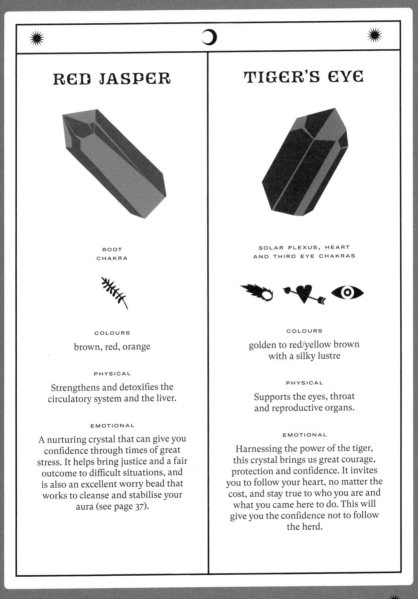

RED JASPER

ROOT
CHAKRA

COLOURS
brown, red, orange

PHYSICAL
Strengthens and detoxifies the
circulatory system and the liver.

EMOTIONAL
A nurturing crystal that can give you
confidence through times of great
stress. It helps bring justice and a fair
outcome to difficult situations, and
is also an excellent worry bead that
works to cleanse and stabilise your
aura (see page 37).

TIGER'S EYE

SOLAR PLEXUS, HEART
AND THIRD EYE CHAKRAS

COLOURS
golden to red/yellow brown
with a silky lustre

PHYSICAL
Supports the eyes, throat
and reproductive organs.

EMOTIONAL
Harnessing the power of the tiger,
this crystal brings us great courage,
protection and confidence. It invites
you to follow your heart, no matter the
cost, and stay true to who you are and
what you came here to do. This will
give you the confidence not to follow
the herd.

CRYSTALS FOR HEALTH

Our health is integral to how we feel about ourselves and how we experience our day-to-day life. You may have a physical illness or accident from which you need to recover or convalesce; sometimes your mental health can be shaky or fail you – and the two often work in tandem. There are also days when you need to boost your health to avoid problems, all of which can be supported by the use of crystals.

You will know where you want to focus your intention and what you want to manifest when it comes to accessing the properties of the eight crystals selected here for health. Make sure you are clear on your intention (see page 66) before you start.

AMETRINE

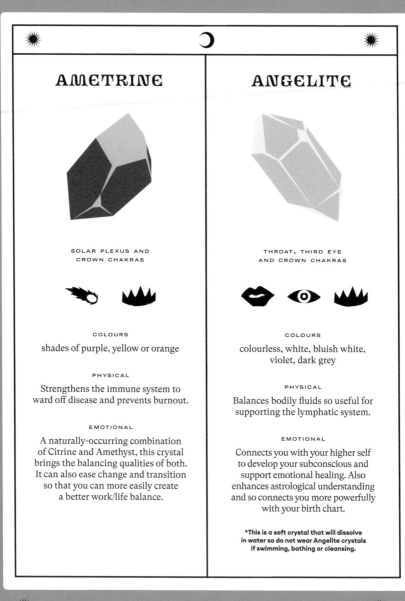

SOLAR PLEXUS AND
CROWN CHAKRAS

COLOURS
shades of purple, yellow or orange

PHYSICAL
Strengthens the immune system to
ward off disease and prevents burnout.

EMOTIONAL
A naturally-occurring combination
of Citrine and Amethyst, this crystal
brings the balancing qualities of both.
It can also ease change and transition
so that you can more easily create
a better work/life balance.

ANGELITE

THROAT, THIRD EYE
AND CROWN CHAKRAS

COLOURS
colourless, white, bluish white,
violet, dark grey

PHYSICAL
Balances bodily fluids so useful for
supporting the lymphatic system.

EMOTIONAL
Connects you with your higher self
to develop your subconscious and
support emotional healing. Also
enhances astrological understanding
and so connects you more powerfully
with your birth chart.

***This is a soft crystal that will dissolve
in water so do not wear Angelite crystals
if swimming, bathing or cleansing.**

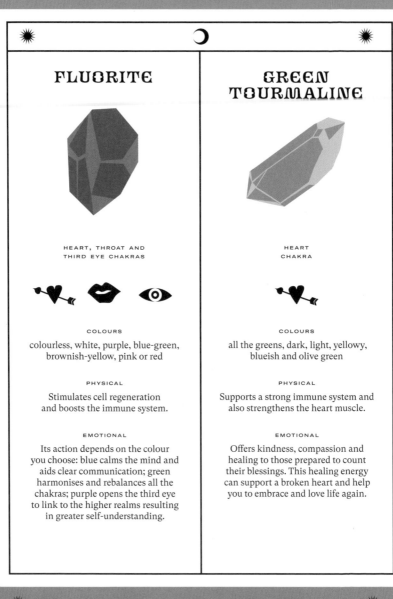

FLUORITE

HEART, THROAT AND
THIRD EYE CHAKRAS

COLOURS
colourless, white, purple, blue-green,
brownish-yellow, pink or red

PHYSICAL
Stimulates cell regeneration
and boosts the immune system.

EMOTIONAL
Its action depends on the colour
you choose: blue calms the mind and
aids clear communication; green
harmonises and rebalances all the
chakras; purple opens the third eye
to link to the higher realms resulting
in greater self-understanding.

GREEN TOURMALINE

HEART
CHAKRA

COLOURS
all the greens, dark, light, yellowy,
blueish and olive green

PHYSICAL
Supports a strong immune system and
also strengthens the heart muscle.

EMOTIONAL
Offers kindness, compassion and
healing to those prepared to count
their blessings. This healing energy
can support a broken heart and help
you to embrace and love life again.

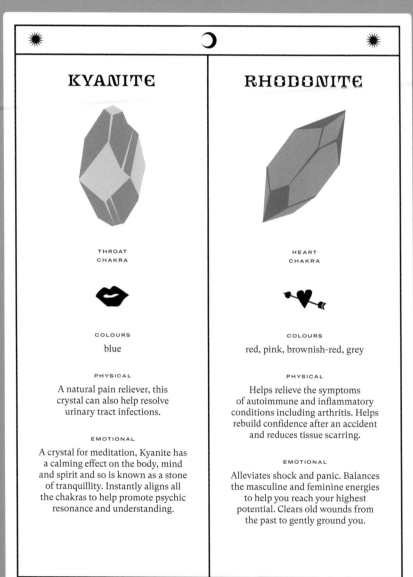

KYANITE

THROAT
CHAKRA

COLOURS
blue

PHYSICAL

A natural pain reliever, this
crystal can also help resolve
urinary tract infections.

EMOTIONAL

A crystal for meditation, Kyanite has
a calming effect on the body, mind
and spirit and so is known as a stone
of tranquillity. Instantly aligns all
the chakras to help promote psychic
resonance and understanding.

RHODONITE

HEART
CHAKRA

COLOURS
red, pink, brownish-red, grey

PHYSICAL

Helps relieve the symptoms
of autoimmune and inflammatory
conditions including arthritis. Helps
rebuild confidence after an accident
and reduces tissue scarring.

EMOTIONAL

Alleviates shock and panic. Balances
the masculine and feminine energies
to help you reach your highest
potential. Clears old wounds from
the past to gently ground you.

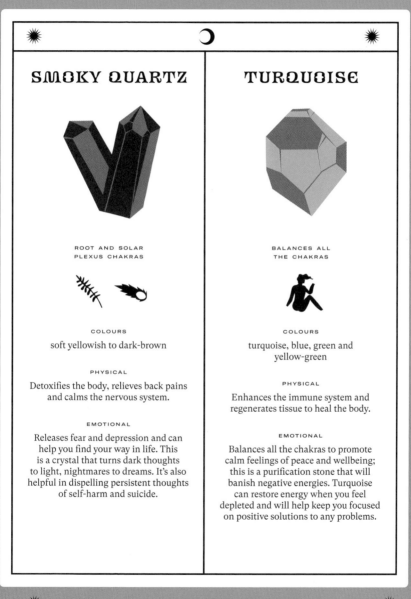

SMOKY QUARTZ

ROOT AND SOLAR
PLEXUS CHAKRAS

COLOURS
soft yellowish to dark-brown

PHYSICAL
Detoxifies the body, relieves back pains
and calms the nervous system.

EMOTIONAL
Releases fear and depression and can
help you find your way in life. This
is a crystal that turns dark thoughts
to light, nightmares to dreams. It's also
helpful in dispelling persistent thoughts
of self-harm and suicide.

TURQUOISE

BALANCES ALL
THE CHAKRAS

COLOURS
turquoise, blue, green and
yellow-green

PHYSICAL
Enhances the immune system and
regenerates tissue to heal the body.

EMOTIONAL
Balances all the chakras to promote
calm feelings of peace and wellbeing;
this is a purification stone that will
banish negative energies. Turquoise
can restore energy when you feel
depleted and will help keep you focused
on positive solutions to any problems.

CRYSTALS FOR CREATIVITY

Creativity comes in all sorts of forms. Sometimes you need to expand your possibilities by thinking or working more creatively – there may be a specific outcome you desire or you may just need to shake things up or remove self-imposed barriers. Either way, creativity in thinking and doing lies at the heart of many of our successes in life, so it pays to pay attention to it.

You will know where you want to focus your intention and what you want to manifest when it comes to accessing the properties of the eight crystals selected here for creativity. Make sure you are clear on your intention (see page 66) before you start.

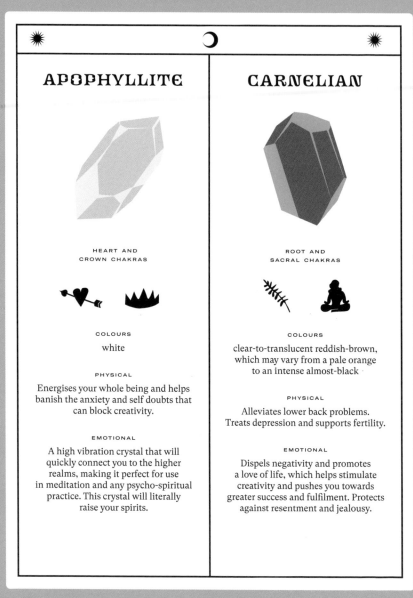

APOPHYLLITE

HEART AND CROWN CHAKRAS

COLOURS

white

PHYSICAL

Energises your whole being and helps banish the anxiety and self doubts that can block creativity.

EMOTIONAL

A high vibration crystal that will quickly connect you to the higher realms, making it perfect for use in meditation and any psycho-spiritual practice. This crystal will literally raise your spirits.

CARNELIAN

ROOT AND SACRAL CHAKRAS

COLOURS

clear-to-translucent reddish-brown, which may vary from a pale orange to an intense almost-black

PHYSICAL

Alleviates lower back problems. Treats depression and supports fertility.

EMOTIONAL

Dispels negativity and promotes a love of life, which helps stimulate creativity and pushes you towards greater success and fulfilment. Protects against resentment and jealousy.

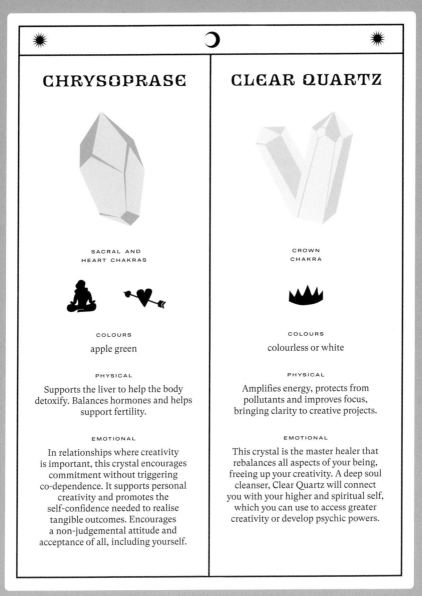

CHRYSOPRASE

SACRAL AND
HEART CHAKRAS

COLOURS

apple green

PHYSICAL

Supports the liver to help the body detoxify. Balances hormones and helps support fertility.

EMOTIONAL

In relationships where creativity is important, this crystal encourages commitment without triggering co-dependence. It supports personal creativity and promotes the self-confidence needed to realise tangible outcomes. Encourages a non-judgemental attitude and acceptance of all, including yourself.

CLEAR QUARTZ

CROWN
CHAKRA

COLOURS

colourless or white

PHYSICAL

Amplifies energy, protects from pollutants and improves focus, bringing clarity to creative projects.

EMOTIONAL

This crystal is the master healer that rebalances all aspects of your being, freeing up your creativity. A deep soul cleanser, Clear Quartz will connect you with your higher and spiritual self, which you can use to access greater creativity or develop psychic powers.

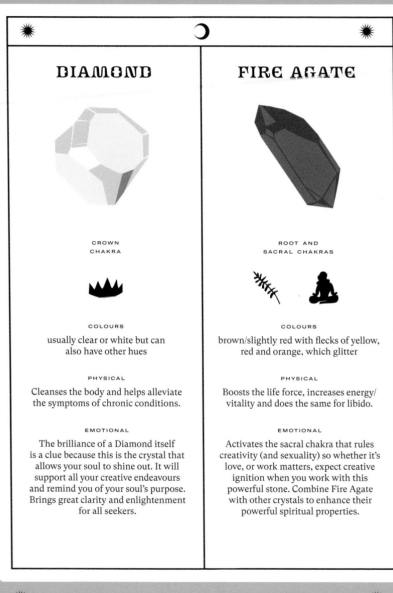

DIAMOND

CROWN CHAKRA

COLOURS

usually clear or white but can
also have other hues

PHYSICAL

Cleanses the body and helps alleviate
the symptoms of chronic conditions.

EMOTIONAL

The brilliance of a Diamond itself
is a clue because this is the crystal that
allows your soul to shine out. It will
support all your creative endeavours
and remind you of your soul's purpose.
Brings great clarity and enlightenment
for all seekers.

FIRE AGATE

ROOT AND SACRAL CHAKRAS

COLOURS

brown/slightly red with flecks of yellow,
red and orange, which glitter

PHYSICAL

Boosts the life force, increases energy/
vitality and does the same for libido.

EMOTIONAL

Activates the sacral chakra that rules
creativity (and sexuality) so whether it's
love, or work matters, expect creative
ignition when you work with this
powerful stone. Combine Fire Agate
with other crystals to enhance their
powerful spiritual properties.

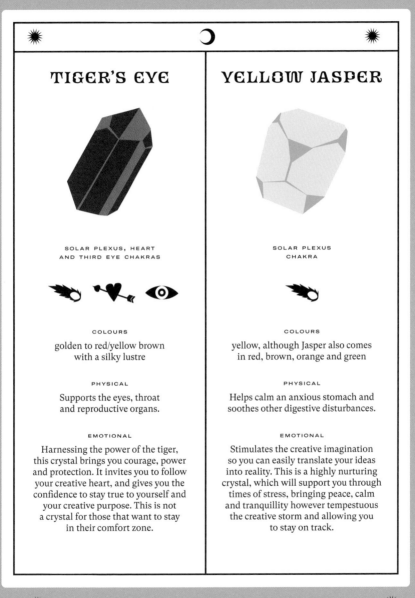

TIGER'S EYE

SOLAR PLEXUS, HEART
AND THIRD EYE CHAKRAS

COLOURS

golden to red/yellow brown
with a silky lustre

PHYSICAL

Supports the eyes, throat
and reproductive organs.

EMOTIONAL

Harnessing the power of the tiger,
this crystal brings you courage, power
and protection. It invites you to follow
your creative heart, and gives you the
confidence to stay true to yourself and
your creative purpose. This is not
a crystal for those that want to stay
in their comfort zone.

YELLOW JASPER

SOLAR PLEXUS
CHAKRA

COLOURS

yellow, although Jasper also comes
in red, brown, orange and green

PHYSICAL

Helps calm an anxious stomach and
soothes other digestive disturbances.

EMOTIONAL

Stimulates the creative imagination
so you can easily translate your ideas
into reality. This is a highly nurturing
crystal, which will support you through
times of stress, bringing peace, calm
and tranquillity however tempestuous
the creative storm and allowing you
to stay on track.

CRYSTALS FOR WORK SUCCESS

Work success often comes from sheer diligence and often by the strategic application of skills, experience and expertise. Sometimes it's not easy to see what the next steps to work success might be and clarification is needed; whether it's in identifying a complete change or need for promotion, selective crystals can help release the energy you need.

You will know where you want to focus your intention and what you want to manifest when it comes to accessing the properties of the eight crystals selected here for work success. Make sure you are clear on your intention (see page 66) before you start.

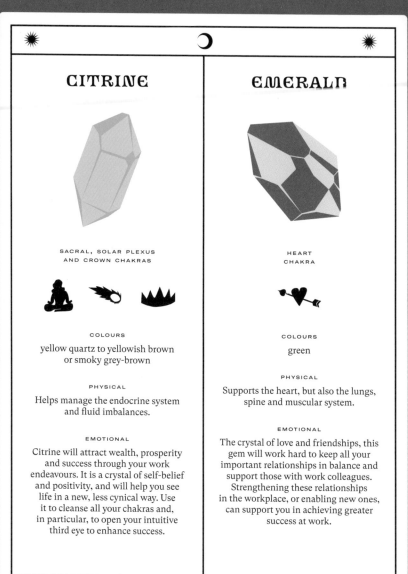

CITRINE

SACRAL, SOLAR PLEXUS
AND CROWN CHAKRAS

COLOURS

yellow quartz to yellowish brown
or smoky grey-brown

PHYSICAL

Helps manage the endocrine system
and fluid imbalances.

EMOTIONAL

Citrine will attract wealth, prosperity
and success through your work
endeavours. It is a crystal of self-belief
and positivity, and will help you see
life in a new, less cynical way. Use
it to cleanse all your chakras and,
in particular, to open your intuitive
third eye to enhance success.

EMERALD

HEART
CHAKRA

COLOURS

green

PHYSICAL

Supports the heart, but also the lungs,
spine and muscular system.

EMOTIONAL

The crystal of love and friendships, this
gem will work hard to keep all your
important relationships in balance and
support those with work colleagues.
Strengthening these relationships
in the workplace, or enabling new ones,
can support you in achieving greater
success at work.

GALENA

ROOT
CHAKRA

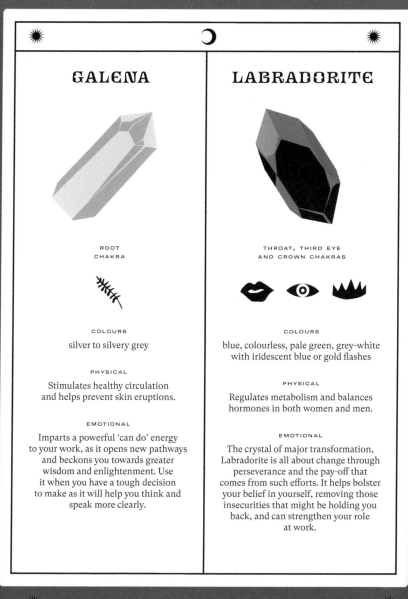

COLOURS

silver to silvery grey

PHYSICAL

Stimulates healthy circulation
and helps prevent skin eruptions.

EMOTIONAL

Imparts a powerful 'can do' energy
to your work, as it opens new pathways
and beckons you towards greater
wisdom and enlightenment. Use
it when you have a tough decision
to make as it will help you think and
speak more clearly.

LABRADORITE

THROAT, THIRD EYE
AND CROWN CHAKRAS

COLOURS

blue, colourless, pale green, grey-white
with iridescent blue or gold flashes

PHYSICAL

Regulates metabolism and balances
hormones in both women and men.

EMOTIONAL

The crystal of major transformation,
Labradorite is all about change through
perseverance and the pay-off that
comes from such efforts. It helps bolster
your belief in yourself, removing those
insecurities that might be holding you
back, and can strengthen your role
at work.

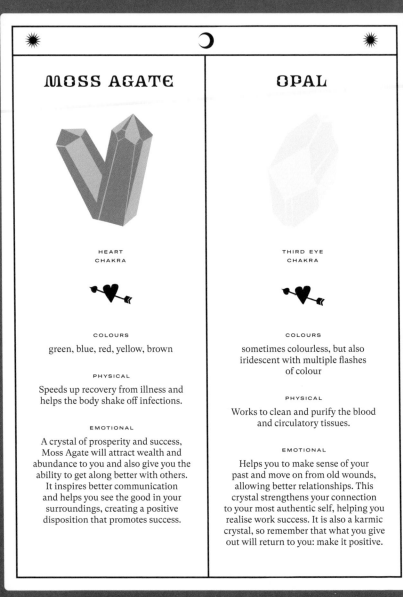

MOSS AGATE

HEART
CHAKRA

COLOURS

green, blue, red, yellow, brown

PHYSICAL

Speeds up recovery from illness and helps the body shake off infections.

EMOTIONAL

A crystal of prosperity and success, Moss Agate will attract wealth and abundance to you and also give you the ability to get along better with others. It inspires better communication and helps you see the good in your surroundings, creating a positive disposition that promotes success.

OPAL

THIRD EYE
CHAKRA

COLOURS

sometimes colourless, but also iridescent with multiple flashes of colour

PHYSICAL

Works to clean and purify the blood and circulatory tissues.

EMOTIONAL

Helps you to make sense of your past and move on from old wounds, allowing better relationships. This crystal strengthens your connection to your most authentic self, helping you realise work success. It is also a karmic crystal, so remember that what you give out will return to you: make it positive.

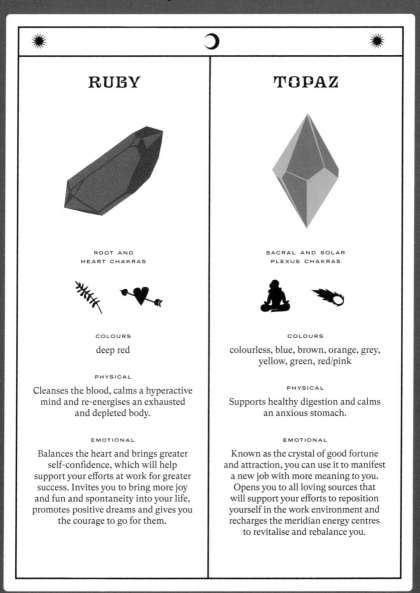

RUBY

ROOT AND
HEART CHAKRAS

COLOURS

deep red

PHYSICAL

Cleanses the blood, calms a hyperactive
mind and re-energises an exhausted
and depleted body.

EMOTIONAL

Balances the heart and brings greater
self-confidence, which will help
support your efforts at work for greater
success. Invites you to bring more joy
and fun and spontaneity into your life,
promotes positive dreams and gives you
the courage to go for them.

TOPAZ

SACRAL AND SOLAR
PLEXUS CHAKRAS

COLOURS

colourless, blue, brown, orange, grey,
yellow, green, red/pink

PHYSICAL

Supports healthy digestion and calms
an anxious stomach.

EMOTIONAL

Known as the crystal of good fortune
and attraction, you can use it to manifest
a new job with more meaning to you.
Opens you to all loving sources that
will support your efforts to reposition
yourself in the work environment and
recharges the meridian energy centres
to revitalise and rebalance you.

CRYSTALS FOR HAPPINESS

It is often said that happiness should be less of an ambition and more of a state of grace, and that often means looking with gratitude at what you already have to help you realise more of what you want. Sometimes our discontent can blind us to the sources of happiness available to us, and the crystals can guide us when we are dealing with the causes of our unhappiness.

You will know where you want to focus your intention and what you want to manifest when it comes to accessing the properties of the eight crystals selected here for happiness. Make sure you are clear on your intention (see page 66) before you start.

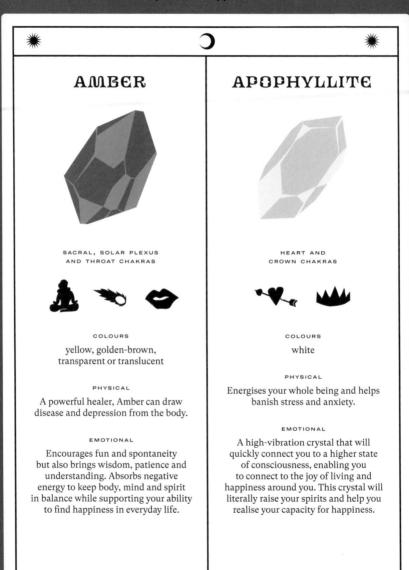

AMBER

SACRAL, SOLAR PLEXUS
AND THROAT CHAKRAS

COLOURS

yellow, golden-brown,
transparent or translucent

PHYSICAL

A powerful healer, Amber can draw
disease and depression from the body.

EMOTIONAL

Encourages fun and spontaneity
but also brings wisdom, patience and
understanding. Absorbs negative
energy to keep body, mind and spirit
in balance while supporting your ability
to find happiness in everyday life.

APOPHYLLITE

HEART AND
CROWN CHAKRAS

COLOURS

white

PHYSICAL

Energises your whole being and helps
banish stress and anxiety.

EMOTIONAL

A high-vibration crystal that will
quickly connect you to a higher state
of consciousness, enabling you
to connect to the joy of living and
happiness around you. This crystal will
literally raise your spirits and help you
realise your capacity for happiness.

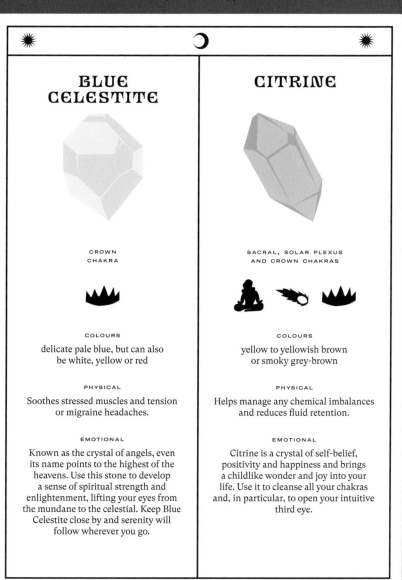

BLUE CELESTITE

CROWN
CHAKRA

COLOURS

delicate pale blue, but can also
be white, yellow or red

PHYSICAL

Soothes stressed muscles and tension
or migraine headaches.

EMOTIONAL

Known as the crystal of angels, even
its name points to the highest of the
heavens. Use this stone to develop
a sense of spiritual strength and
enlightenment, lifting your eyes from
the mundane to the celestial. Keep Blue
Celestite close by and serenity will
follow wherever you go.

CITRINE

SACRAL, SOLAR PLEXUS
AND CROWN CHAKRAS

COLOURS

yellow to yellowish brown
or smoky grey-brown

PHYSICAL

Helps manage any chemical imbalances
and reduces fluid retention.

EMOTIONAL

Citrine is a crystal of self-belief,
positivity and happiness and brings
a childlike wonder and joy into your
life. Use it to cleanse all your chakras
and, in particular, to open your intuitive
third eye.

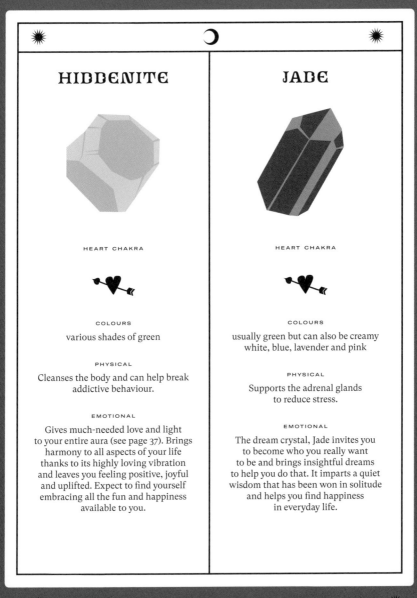

HIDDENITE

HEART CHAKRA

COLOURS
various shades of green

PHYSICAL
Cleanses the body and can help break addictive behaviour.

EMOTIONAL
Gives much-needed love and light to your entire aura (see page 37). Brings harmony to all aspects of your life thanks to its highly loving vibration and leaves you feeling positive, joyful and uplifted. Expect to find yourself embracing all the fun and happiness available to you.

JADE

HEART CHAKRA

COLOURS
usually green but can also be creamy white, blue, lavender and pink

PHYSICAL
Supports the adrenal glands to reduce stress.

EMOTIONAL
The dream crystal, Jade invites you to become who you really want to be and brings insightful dreams to help you do that. It imparts a quiet wisdom that has been won in solitude and helps you find happiness in everyday life.

PURPLE AMETHYST

THIRD EYE AND
CROWN CHAKRAS

COLOURS

purple but can also be a pinky
violet colour

PHYSICAL

Regulates hormones by fine-tuning
the entire endocrine system.

EMOTIONAL

A natural tranquilliser, Amethyst can
dissolve negativity to help alleviate
feelings of sadness, grief and despair,
freeing you up to a happier state
of mind. It also encourages spiritual
growth and can activate any latent
psychic abilities.

YELLOW JASPER

SOLAR PLEXUS
CHAKRA

COLOURS

yellow, although Jasper also comes
in red, brown, orange and green

PHYSICAL

Helps calm an upset stomach and
soothes other digestive disturbances.

EMOTIONAL

Stimulates the imagination so you can
easily translate your ideas into your
reality. This is a highly nurturing stone
that will support you through times
of extreme stress, bringing peace
and calm and tranquillity, however
tempestuous a storm you are facing.

CRYSTALS FOR FERTILITY

The creation of new life doesn't always come easily and there may be reasons why the body and mind resists this form of creativity. Unblocking and rebalancing energy in the body may be a useful first step when fertility is at issue and the vibrational properties of many crystals can help with the realignment of the internal environment to help achieve conception.

You will know where you want to focus your intention and what you want to manifest when it comes to accessing the properties of the eight crystals selected here for fertility. Make sure you are clear on your intention (see page 66) before you start.

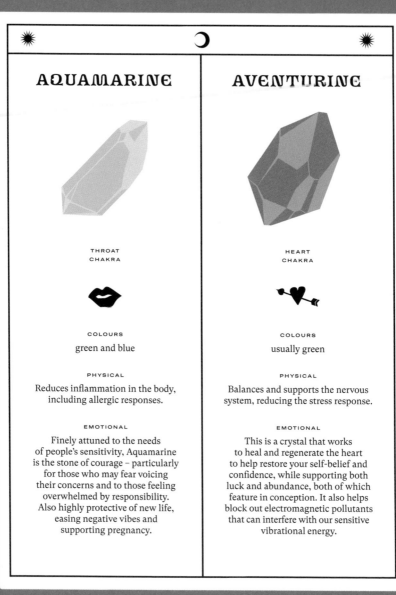

AQUAMARINE

THROAT
CHAKRA

COLOURS
green and blue

PHYSICAL
Reduces inflammation in the body,
including allergic responses.

EMOTIONAL
Finely attuned to the needs
of people's sensitivity, Aquamarine
is the stone of courage – particularly
for those who may fear voicing
their concerns and to those feeling
overwhelmed by responsibility.
Also highly protective of new life,
easing negative vibes and
supporting pregnancy.

AVENTURINE

HEART
CHAKRA

COLOURS
usually green

PHYSICAL
Balances and supports the nervous
system, reducing the stress response.

EMOTIONAL
This is a crystal that works
to heal and regenerate the heart
to help restore your self-belief and
confidence, while supporting both
luck and abundance, both of which
feature in conception. It also helps
block out electromagnetic pollutants
that can interfere with our sensitive
vibrational energy.

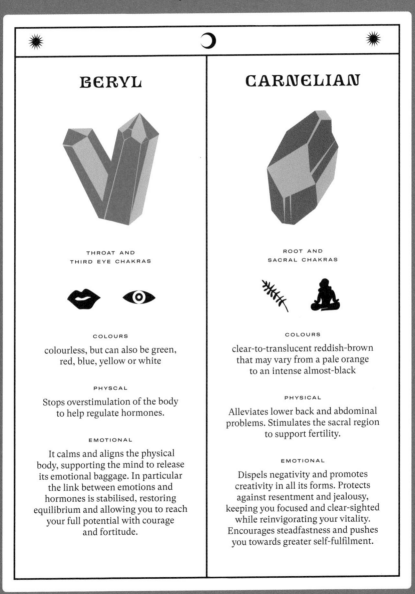

BERYL

THROAT AND
THIRD EYE CHAKRAS

COLOURS

colourless, but can also be green,
red, blue, yellow or white

PHYSCAL

Stops overstimulation of the body
to help regulate hormones.

EMOTIONAL

It calms and aligns the physical
body, supporting the mind to release
its emotional baggage. In particular
the link between emotions and
hormones is stabilised, restoring
equilibrium and allowing you to reach
your full potential with courage
and fortitude.

CARNELIAN

ROOT AND
SACRAL CHAKRAS

COLOURS

clear-to-translucent reddish-brown
that may vary from a pale orange
to an intense almost-black

PHYSICAL

Alleviates lower back and abdominal
problems. Stimulates the sacral region
to support fertility.

EMOTIONAL

Dispels negativity and promotes
creativity in all its forms. Protects
against resentment and jealousy,
keeping you focused and clear-sighted
while reinvigorating your vitality.
Encourages steadfastness and pushes
you towards greater self-fulfilment.

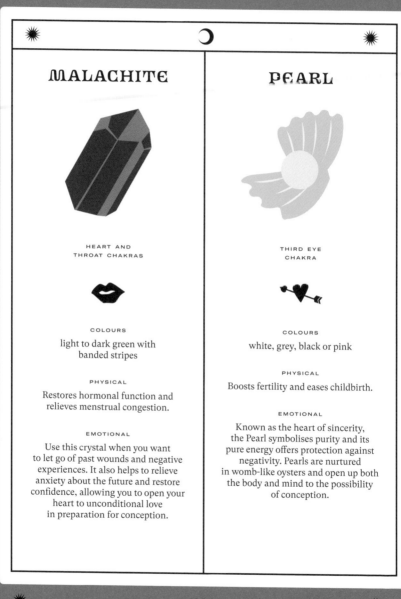

MALACHITE

HEART AND
THROAT CHAKRAS

COLOURS

light to dark green with
banded stripes

PHYSICAL

Restores hormonal function and
relieves menstrual congestion.

EMOTIONAL

Use this crystal when you want
to let go of past wounds and negative
experiences. It also helps to relieve
anxiety about the future and restore
confidence, allowing you to open your
heart to unconditional love
in preparation for conception.

PEARL

THIRD EYE
CHAKRA

COLOURS

white, grey, black or pink

PHYSICAL

Boosts fertility and eases childbirth.

EMOTIONAL

Known as the heart of sincerity,
the Pearl symbolises purity and its
pure energy offers protection against
negativity. Pearls are nurtured
in womb-like oysters and open up both
the body and mind to the possibility
of conception.

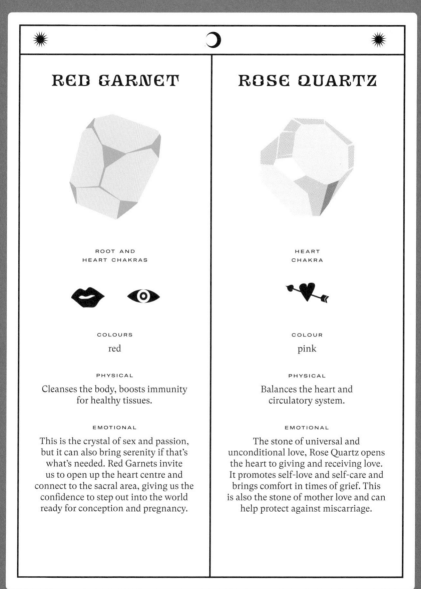

RED GARNET

ROOT AND
HEART CHAKRAS

COLOURS

red

PHYSICAL

Cleanses the body, boosts immunity
for healthy tissues.

EMOTIONAL

This is the crystal of sex and passion,
but it can also bring serenity if that's
what's needed. Red Garnets invite
us to open up the heart centre and
connect to the sacral area, giving us the
confidence to step out into the world
ready for conception and pregnancy.

ROSE QUARTZ

HEART
CHAKRA

COLOUR

pink

PHYSICAL

Balances the heart and
circulatory system.

EMOTIONAL

The stone of universal and
unconditional love, Rose Quartz opens
the heart to giving and receiving love.
It promotes self-love and self-care and
brings comfort in times of grief. This
is also the stone of mother love and can
help protect against miscarriage.

CRYSTALS FOR PROTECTION

A sense of unease can be very troubling and sometimes we feel the need for protection from our surroundings or from our own worst imaginings. Feeling at ease in yourself and your environment can be enhanced by those protective crystal energies available to you, helping to manifest a more secure state, both psychic and physical, in which to live.

You will know where you want to focus your intention and what you want to manifest when it comes to accessing the properties of the eight crystals selected here for protection. Make sure you are clear on your intention (see page 66) before you start.

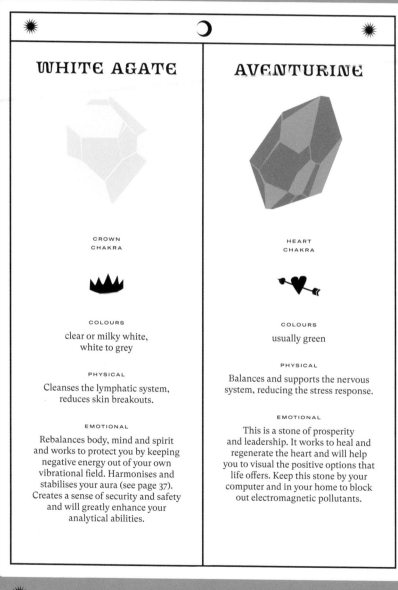

WHITE AGATE

CROWN
CHAKRA

COLOURS
clear or milky white,
white to grey

PHYSICAL
Cleanses the lymphatic system,
reduces skin breakouts.

EMOTIONAL
Rebalances body, mind and spirit
and works to protect you by keeping
negative energy out of your own
vibrational field. Harmonises and
stabilises your aura (see page 37).
Creates a sense of security and safety
and will greatly enhance your
analytical abilities.

AVENTURINE

HEART
CHAKRA

COLOURS
usually green

PHYSICAL
Balances and supports the nervous
system, reducing the stress response.

EMOTIONAL
This is a stone of prosperity
and leadership. It works to heal and
regenerate the heart and will help
you to visual the positive options that
life offers. Keep this stone by your
computer and in your home to block
out electromagnetic pollutants.

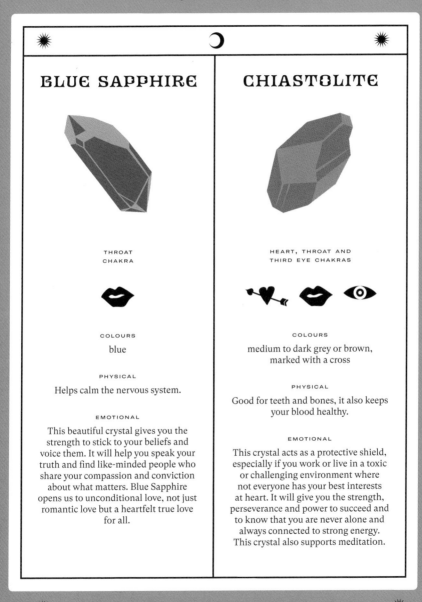

BLUE SAPPHIRE

THROAT
CHAKRA

COLOURS
blue

PHYSICAL
Helps calm the nervous system.

EMOTIONAL
This beautiful crystal gives you the strength to stick to your beliefs and voice them. It will help you speak your truth and find like-minded people who share your compassion and conviction about what matters. Blue Sapphire opens us to unconditional love, not just romantic love but a heartfelt true love for all.

CHIASTOLITE

HEART, THROAT AND
THIRD EYE CHAKRAS

COLOURS
medium to dark grey or brown, marked with a cross

PHYSICAL
Good for teeth and bones, it also keeps your blood healthy.

EMOTIONAL
This crystal acts as a protective shield, especially if you work or live in a toxic or challenging environment where not everyone has your best interests at heart. It will give you the strength, perseverance and power to succeed and to know that you are never alone and always connected to strong energy. This crystal also supports meditation.

CHALCEDONY

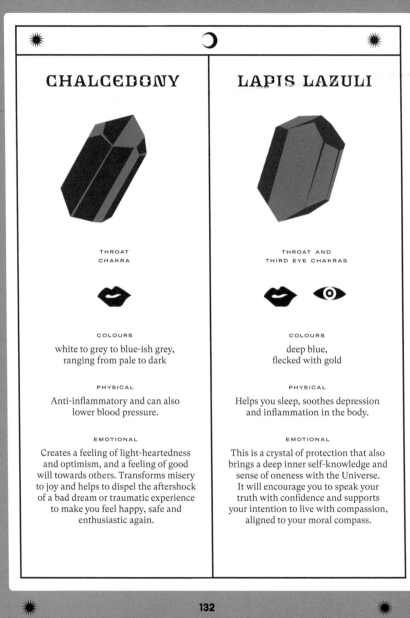

THROAT
CHAKRA

COLOURS

white to grey to blue-ish grey,
ranging from pale to dark

PHYSICAL

Anti-inflammatory and can also
lower blood pressure.

EMOTIONAL

Creates a feeling of light-heartedness
and optimism, and a feeling of good
will towards others. Transforms misery
to joy and helps to dispel the aftershock
of a bad dream or traumatic experience
to make you feel happy, safe and
enthusiastic again.

LAPIS LAZULI

THROAT AND
THIRD EYE CHAKRAS

COLOURS

deep blue,
flecked with gold

PHYSICAL

Helps you sleep, soothes depression
and inflammation in the body.

EMOTIONAL

This is a crystal of protection that also
brings a deep inner self-knowledge and
sense of oneness with the Universe.
It will encourage you to speak your
truth with confidence and supports
your intention to live with compassion,
aligned to your moral compass.

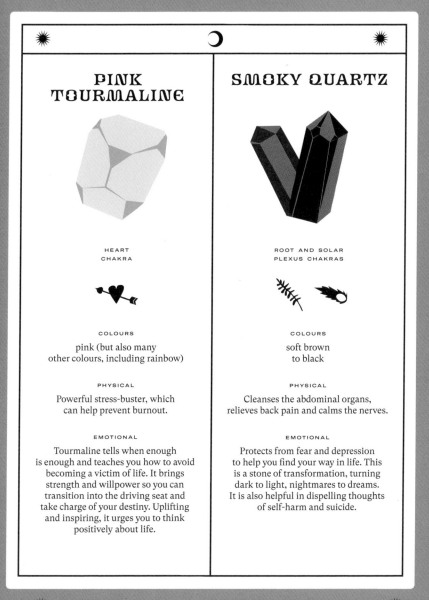

PINK TOURMALINE

HEART
CHAKRA

COLOURS
pink (but also many
other colours, including rainbow)

PHYSICAL
Powerful stress-buster, which
can help prevent burnout.

EMOTIONAL
Tourmaline tells when enough
is enough and teaches you how to avoid
becoming a victim of life. It brings
strength and willpower so you can
transition into the driving seat and
take charge of your destiny. Uplifting
and inspiring, it urges you to think
positively about life.

SMOKY QUARTZ

ROOT AND SOLAR
PLEXUS CHAKRAS

COLOURS
soft brown
to black

PHYSICAL
Cleanses the abdominal organs,
relieves back pain and calms the nerves.

EMOTIONAL
Protects from fear and depression
to help you find your way in life. This
is a stone of transformation, turning
dark to light, nightmares to dreams.
It is also helpful in dispelling thoughts
of self-harm and suicide.

INDEX

A

abundance 69, 112, 124
acceptance 105
addictive behaviour 119
adrenal glands 119
affirmations 32–5
agate 25, 57
    fire agate 20, 88
    moss agate 22, 112
    white agate 130
aims
    clarity about 64–5
    setting intentions 66
allergic responses 124
amber 22, 24, 35, 57, 116
amethysts 32, 58
    purple amethysts 25, 120
ametrine 23, 94
analytical abilities 130
angelite 25, 94
anger, soothing 58
animal shapes 53
anxiety 102, 107, 113, 116, 126
apophyllite 21, 102, 116
aquamarine 25, 124
Aquarius 25
Aries 20
arrow shaped crystals 53
arthritis 98
astral plane 39
astrology 17–25, 94
    and energy 20, 21
attraction, law of 13–14, 48
aura 37–41, 119, 130
aural planes 38–41
authenticity 9, 13, 112
autoimmune diseases 98
aventurine 20, 34, 58, 80, 124, 130

B

back pain 99, 102, 125, 133
balancing 81, 83, 89, 116
    chakras 99
    hormones 89, 105, 111, 120
bathrooms 57
bedrooms 57
beryl 23, 125
birth signs 18–25
blood. *see* circulatory system
blood pressure 132
blue celestite 25, 33, 51, 117
blue crystals 54
blue sapphires 22
the body 38
bones 131

C

calm(ing) 98, 120, 125
    colours 54, 96
    digestion 107, 113, 120
    the mind 63, 96, 113
    nervous system 99, 131, 133
    palm stones 53
Cancer 21
Capricorn 24
caring for crystals 61
carnelian 20, 35, 59, 125
causal plane 40
celestial plane 40
celestite, blue 25, 33, 51, 117
cell regeneration 96
chakras 27
    aligning 98
    balancing 99
    cleansing 88, 110, 117

B

Index

ACKNOWLEDGEMENTS

Many thanks are due to the team at Hardie Grant publishers for their continued support and commitment to my work, in particular Kate Burkett and Eila Purvis. Evi O Studio's talents as illustrator and designer have made this book beautiful, as with all my other books.

ABOUT THE AUTHOR

Stella Andromeda is an astrologer and author of the internationally bestselling series of 12 Zodiac titles *Seeing Stars*, along with *Love Match*, *Cat Astrology*, *Dog Astrology*, *AstroBirthdays*, *AstroAffirmations* and *Wise Cat Tarot*, also published by Hardie Grant. Her fascination with crystals is aligned to her knowledge of astrology, and in *AstroCrystals* she celebrates their use in manifesting your hopes and dreams.

Published in 2023 by Hardie Grant Books,
an imprint of Hardie Grant Publishing

Hardie Grant Books (London)
5th & 6th Floors
52–54 Southwark Street
London SE1 1UN

Hardie Grant Books (Melbourne)
Building 1, 658 Church Street
Richmond, Victoria 3121
hardiegrantbooks.com

British Library Cataloguing-in-Publication Data.
A catalogue record for this book is available from the British Library.

AstroCrystals
ISBN: 978-1-78488-637-0

10 9 8 7 6 5 4 3 2 1

Publishing Director: Kajal Mistry
Acting Publishing Director: Emma Hopkin
Commissioning Editor: Kate Burkett
Senior Editor: Eila Purvis
Design: Evi-O.Studio | Emi Chiba
Illustrations: Evi-O.Studio | Emi Chiba, Marcus Cheong & Siena Zadro
Copy-editor: Marie Clayton
Proofreader: Susan Clark
Indexer: Cathy Heath
Production Controller: Martina Georgieva

Colour reproduction by p2d
Printed and bound in China by Leo Paper Products Ltd.